A GOOD TIME
HAD BY ALL

A GOOD TIME HAD BY ALL

Meaghan Strimas

Exile Editions

Publishers of singular
Fiction, Poetry, Translation, Drama, and Nonfiction

2010

Library and Archives Canada Cataloguing in Publication

Strimas, Meaghan, 1977-
    A good time had by all / Meaghan Strimas.

Poems.

ISBN 978-1-55096-140-9

    I. Title.

PS8637.T76G66 2010   C811'.6   C2010-900777-8

Front Cover Photo/Design Jeannette Lorito
Back Cover faded paper with floral pattern Bill Noll
Design and Composition by Digital ReproSet
Typeset in Big Caslon and Garamond fonts at the Moons of Jupiter Studios
Printed in Canada by Imprimerie Gauvin

The publisher would like to acknowledge the financial assistance of
the Canada Council for the Arts and the Ontario Arts Council, which is
an agency of the Government of Ontario.

 Conseil des Arts   Canada Council
du Canada   for the Arts    ONTARIO ARTS COUNCIL
                                          CONSEIL DES ARTS DE L'ONTARIO

Published in Canada in 2010 by Exile Editions Ltd.
144483 Southgate Road 14 ~ Gen Del
Holstein, Ontario, N0G 2A0
info@exileeditions.com
www.ExileEditions.com

Canadian Sales Distribution: U.S. Sales Distribution:
McArthur & Company   Independent Publishers Group
c/o Harper Collins   814 North Franklin Street
1995 Markham Road   Chicago, IL 60610
Toronto, ON M1B 5M8   www.ipgbook.com
toll free: 1 800 387 0117   toll free: 1 800 888 4741

For
Norma & John,
Betty & Mac.

CONTENTS

REVERENCE, LIFE

LADIES & GENTLEMEN

GNOME, SWEET GNOME
(A SUITE OF POEMS)

LOVE, DELIVERANCE

The art of losing isn't hard to master.

—Elizabeth Bishop

REVERENCE, LIFE

Nod to the Drunkard I Once
Sat Next to in the Park

Well, here we are comes to mind
though I do not say it. As here you are,
pissed drunk at noon & stinking of piss
& booze, heavenly booze & you're likely
randy, though gentleman enough
not to touch or make mention of the woman
next to you on this bench. I'm lunching
& lonely. I'd like to chuck my ham sandwich
across the park just to see the pigeons flock.

My drunkard friend, miracle that you are,
singular, you will never happen again, much
as I won't happen again, but loathe, we so
often do, this singularity. If open rebuke
is of greater virtue than love concealed, I'm weak.
What we share is silence & in this moment,
I see you turn from green to gilt to gold,
you who are, unwittingly, thankfully,
in this moment, my Angel of Repose.

The Spirit
for Evie

No two more surly than you & I,
we out-shot the old boys, *Chugged! Chugged!*
'til I nearly burst an eye. One dire
soul–s*teady*–sparked a ciggy wrong-end-
round, roared at me, *Liquor in the front
& poker in the rear*, his Rebel Song.

✳

Head turning, your hair met fire. Struck,
I watched a lock furl, shrivel, but no
matter. *Oh*, we proclaimed, *it's rye!*
when Mr. Bartender tipped a jigger.

✳

First altarlight of sun, drivel rolled
off our tongues: *What have we done?*
Tenuous levity tumbled. Betrayed,
we wept like children lost in woods. For
every demon excised, two more planted.

Requiem–Let the Angels
Rise from Piggy's Palace

for Sereena Abotsway & Others

Mercy. Mercy. Is it morning?

Has the farmer wakened?
Has he slept? Or have the circling
angels left him restless?

✻

Those are his cloven hooves
unfastening the latch. That is his pitchfork
heart, a lantern creeping through the stalks.
The scarecrow begs the birds to rest:
Here. Land. Let me host your holy nest.

The creature skulks, lopsidedly, toward
the barn, & the sparkling field of frost
begins to thaw. He stops &, kneeling, peers
into the bucket as if into a well. A severed head
with eyes of green. Her hair is brown.
Black mascara smeared across her cheeks.

He'll pry out her every tooth
& feed her to the sow.

❉

Mercy. Another disappeared.
One more mother, sister, lover
left to ask, *Where is she? Why?*

Or, as likely, the memory of her
dissolved with the final breath. That's that.

Where Are You Billy Spano?

You rat.

You bastard.

    Where are you now?

    (Failing to raise Cain in Limbo?

        For God knows
    Heaven never rang, for you, her gracious bell.)

Remember me, Billy Spano?
Your torturer, tormenter. I'm the girl
who yanked your pants down in the park.
Who called you nasty names
& passed them 'round the lots.

                Where
are you, Little Billy? Little Goat.
Little Man who couldn't tell his left foot
from his right. Weren't you the boy who'd wet
his joggers at the prospect of a fight?

A rat-tat-tattle. A stray.
The Scoundrel, mangy, tethered to a stake,
whose ma forgot

to pack his lunch,
or pat his head,
to say goodbye
the day she finally split. Oh, Billy.

One spring morning I found you tracing
circles on your trike. Far from the clangour
of schoolyard barbs, we scuttled down
a clover-laden hill, caught craws & kissed
the cool white bellies of slow, spy-hopping frogs.

That day I didn't mind your toneless whistling,
outlandish, garbled thoughts, how
you chewed & spat your filthy fingernails.

We were the beginnings of a plot: you + me, Billy S.

Look, you said. *That fella there is flying off the bridge...*
The man's retort, a splat, gore that ran & ran
like water through cupped hands.   Billy. Bill.

A teenager, you'd mimic that same flight, de-winged.

Billy, it was you who leaned in close
(I can hear your ski coat rustling in this dark.
        Your nostrils clogged with snot.)

Never frightened you, that big-shot
death–you came in for the kiss, ruthless.

How We Helm the Deer

The Barrel girl grew from fawn to doe
that year & departed from the race.

She'd gone buck wild with some smart
aleck who would've stuck it in her eye,
ear, air hole. He dicked her in the dark.
Closed his eyes & held his breath. He could
not bare her bleeding gums or coat of stink.
They squeaked atop rusty wheels & a tune
played along: love is a leaky faucet.

At home in their one-and-a-half, the girl's
father slouched, stared at a screen of static
& chugged warm bottles of homemade beer.
A buck's head, nailed to wood veneer,
wondered how it had come to have two
bottle caps plugged into his empty eye
sockets. Glass eyes would've broke the bank.

She'd felt the tear & hoofed, staved,
walked home to graze in his ghost.

To Give, Receive

The crux of conspiracy lies
in the story we choose to believe & the kindly man who
hugs his missal, warns, *Nothing is as it seems.*

The lights tonight are ephemera. The moon,
a scythe in the sky.

My soul drifts, a scrap of paper. Blows ahead
of my feet through endless alleys, dim streets.

Legions beg & beseech as we pass & we pass
them by. I walk within the shops & ask,
What in God's Name should I buy?

We speak of Salvation, the multitude we hope to rise,
but my heart knows little of sacrifice. We gluttons thrive.

Some clown whistles on his blade of grass.
We strut 'round pennies that fall, peck holes in the skulls
of the needy, fan our gall.

Ask & you will receive. Give & you will receive.

What is it, to give nothing & still receive?

Separation / Anxiety

Inherent in our beginnings,
a natural rhythm:
all that communes must diverge.

In birth, separation's inception.
A calf born takes life's first blow.
The red ribbon is cut,
the severance makes whole.
A hoof sears ground. Earth's
cold blanket unfolds.

The search begins. Fails.
In its place, small,
everyday exchanges.
Hello abates goodbye.
Light averts dark.

We are together. We are apart.

I Am?

What we are looking for
is what is looking.
—ST. FRANCIS OF ASSISI

Who is thinking
these thoughts?
I am unable to name
or understand
the creature I am.

I see my hands,
fingers on the keys,
typing, abysmally.

I am the lone breather
in this room
pondering family photos.

I cannot find
a trace of intelligent
design in their faces,
have a harder time
recognizing myself.

Blue shirt in the middle
maybe?

Lost Causes

You turn a blind eye. Lost causes don't merit, I told you so.
I'm spoiled. Turning to curd. A rascal churning out fiascos.
I have my days, but a long list of failure lessens the glow.

I suck on mothballs. I pick my nose. Trivial. Now you know.
Fuck-up. Loser. Face distorted by my mask of pantyhose.
You turn a blind eye. Lost causes don't merit, I told you so.

Have you heard of *Noonday Demon*? A bottomless low?
I wanted to chew its nose off but fell asleep in a sticky hole.
I have my days, but a long list of failure lessens the glow.

Why's the fish catching bird's blood in a bowl? Why does
the beetle sew the shroud? Who wrote this horror show?
Your blind eye turns. My head hurts. Tell me about so and so.

I don't blame you, not really. I'm heavy. Wet wool.
I've drained the sink's dirty water. Wrung the towel.
We had our day. My endless failures lessened the glow.

Let's not say our sorrys. Some day we'll both go cold.
Until then, if my body writes your body & your body doesn't
reply, should my body write your body to ask the reason why?
Never mind. You've turned. Say it. You told me so.

The Devil to Make

I've no deal with the devil
to make: broken many deals, I have.
That's devil-incarnate-enough
for this life. I've nothing. *Nada.*
Blind as the boy playing Jacks
in the street because he doesn't yet
know what trouble he's in.
Big Life will drill his hole
in any heart–best intentions
don't apply. Direction is hell-bent.
The Good Lord went down
in a plane long ago. They're still
searching for that bastard who
served him the last shot.
Forget the infant in his cradle.
He'll meet the same smite
as us bigger beasts. The devil
walks on two feet. He's carrying
daffodils & he carries roses.
Flowers have lost their scent.
The same mistakes we'll make
again. There are no more deals
with the devil to make. So we
fake it. Broken, we wade through.

On the Threshold of Eternity

(after Vincent Van Gogh's Old Man in Sorrow)

Come not my way,
eternity.

What doesn't it mean
to be human?

You ask why my head
is in my hands.
Why I do not look up.

I am lucky, so
I will sit in this chair.

I am lucky enough
to sit here & stare.

Immaterial, I Think

To be egoless, I am told, is to dwell
in love: to give, not receive, with ease.
I have acquaintance with this state,
but I am weak. Judgement, freedom
from it, a greased pig. I should not wonder,
so often, what others think of me. Nor
should you of you. We should be strong.
Dwell in peace. Here, I'll see you to the door.

What difference does it make if I do
not like you, if you do not like me?

LADIES & GENTLEMEN

Once I Was Witness

It's late, or early, depending.
I'd like to tell you I'm not
the lonely type, but here I am, lured,
happily, from a restlessness
by the skirmish of two surly lovers.

Posted by the kitchen window,
I behold the battle–a man,
a woman, both sullied by the bottle.
I'm so sick of you, she rages. In response,
he tries to pull her close.

I think I know this one. The woman
who wants to be loved, but isn't.
The man who wants to love, but doesn't.

A door slams. She's behind
the wheel of their banged-up ride.
He holds on tight to the side mirror.
A *fuck you* later, the car peels away.
He clings, upright. Skitters across the asphalt.

Brakes squeal. I turn. The cat
trills. Back to the window, again.
Asshole, she spits at the thing splayed.

An Old Broad's Belongings

When the old broad, who lived across the road
went *kaput*, I hoped nobody'd refer
to me as "the old broad," & in the sick chambers
of my brain, I wondered if she'd been up there long.

The broad's kids parked haphazardly in her lane.
Hustled from their cars. Two daughters,
garish as Gerber daisies, cleaned house,
while the son, a capital-V virgin, I'm sure,
played with the stake of a For Sale sign.
After several puncture wounds to the lawn, it stood erect.

I'd been to estate sales before, but not like this–
the impression of her lower lip, Violet #21, imprinted
on a goblet (selling for a dime), & the dregs
of her final breath crawling out the door.

Letter to My Sister,
One-time "Downtown Elf"

You hadn't wanted to leave home
but it was the next step–university,
graduation. Later, a paycheque.

Cordoned by your life's belongings
in the back-seat corner
of the family car.
Milk crates and garbage bags
full of dirty laundry
pressed against your body.

The girl's dormitory filled
you with despair. Bloated
macaroni in the bathroom sink.
The hallway heavy
with hairspray and perfume.
Ruckus rounds of laughter
you couldn't comprehend.
Rules of a sport you never played.

You bailed before the holidays.
Called Dad for a lift back home.

There was good news in the mix.
You'd been hired as the town's
"Downtown Elf."

(The stakes were low.
We'd all gone mad. It wasn't you alone.)

You wore an elfin hat. Wandered.
Fed nickels into near-expired
parking meters. Slipped
the courtesy note
under windshield wipers:
Season's Greetings!
You've just been spared a ticket
by the town hall's Downtown Elf.

You made friends
with the self-proclaimed preacher
who'd found God in the YMCA
locker room. The fat lady
who sang carols in Pig Latin.
I prayed you bow to compulsion
at least once & spend
every cold Christmas
nickel at Vern's Donut Villa.

The rush-light of winter
left you in the dark
at the end of each shift.
Guileless, you felt
your way back. Exposure,
however harsh, couldn't match
the loneliness you owned.

Sighting (with Great Aunt Jean)

Eighteen, tongue newly pierced
& ugly with infection, I watch

my grief-gobsmacked Aunt
tread her empty kitchen.

A pitiful portrait. I'll name it,
Jean Moving to the Home.

Still subject to my mother's coaching
(a pinch on my upper arm), I lead

my Aunt, strange lady, down
the lane with the ruse of a walk.

"I'm an avid birder," Jean explains,
straightening her visor.

Each part of her binoculars is
"the dingus." She spit-shines the lenses.

Miles from field or forest when
Jean exclaims, "Crow. Crow."

Say this scene is, *Look, a bird, a plane!*
I shield my eyes and spy

a ribbon of flickering black tape
snagged on a telephone wire.

Man from the Abattoir

Puck's mother, Rita,
was the neighbourhood babysitter.
He was her only son.
In the basement of her home.

A bachelor, we were warned,
was someone to be feared.

He worked at the slaughterhouse.
Boiled hooves made glue.

A couple of us kids would hang
around Puck's door, hoping
he might hear our noise,
invite us for a vid, a soda from his fridge.

When we wrestled him, he'd rub his stink
onto our clothes, afterbirth & sweet cologne.
He let us lick warm whisky from his chin.
Puck taught us how to roll our own.

We loved him.

A collection of old bones & teeth
had been arranged on top his TV.
We held the horse hoof to our ears.
I could never hear the chirrup
of a bird, or the sea.
Puck was sure of both.

The dogs, they loved him too.
The yard of the weathered
wartime was riddled with dog dirt
we'd hop over in the summer,
the steepled piles of shit
slackening in the sprinkler's shower.

Puck wasn't sure if his bird-bird
had died or remarried.
We learned how to furdle photos
of spread-eagle girlies.

Then my mother heard a story,
& Puck, he moved away.

Hot Chicken on a Bun

I was nine & not so bright.
Read it in the town weekly, *fall fair
contest, dog & owner look-a-like.*

Pop said, *No.* Later, *Fine, we'll go.*

I dressed to match Pup's coat.
Pug & hound. Tip-to-toe brown.

After 4-H, before Fancy Hens,
my knees near buckled when we ran
into the big barn's showing ring.

Pup, he faltered. Munched
manure, humped the judge's leg.
I searched the stands
for friendship, Dad's face.

Pop led us to the lot where he took
a pull of Crown & tossed
my yelping mess into the trunk.

I blubbered as we walked back
to the show. Pop squeezed my
hand until it curled into a claw.
Ordered me hot chicken on a bun.

From back row, our rickety perch,
my father cawed.

One golden bird escaped,
picked a fight.

A feather landed on my sandwich.

He hoisted me above the cheering crowd:
Mind, girl, he said. *This here will make you strong.*

Love's Reprobate

The less I visit, the more
I think myself back to your house
I grew up in.
—Andrew Motion

Must be those noiseless children playing in the street
who drag me back his way. Pop's ghost came home today,
half-dart tucked behind his ear. *Howdy, girl. Been years.*
Used to be just me & him, at the table. In the quiet
of the night he'd kill the golden bottle, his heart
grinding out its ruby sludge despite life's ugly failures.
Suppose it's when he'd had enough that he'd rise
to fight the walls, fists breaking up paper & plaster.
Soon after, a mumble or a plea: *Time to get some sleep.*
That's when I'd mope upon the staircase, drop
a useless toy into one of the holes he'd made, hoping
that, from between the walls, it might someday be
freed, mistaken for the remnant of a happy game.

Job Search

I'm good friends
with the pavement I pound.

I'll take anything.

I can't face another day
busted, broke.

I come home.
Check the messages.
My mother.

I brush my teeth.
Look at myself in the mirror.
"Hello, is the manager in?"
rehearsed until
notched in the brain's tuck.

I wake again.

Soon mincing
the hallow-maw of main street,
every crappy drug & dollar store
is a bustle.

The polyester-clad employees dazzle.
I'd kill to wear that navy smock.

And then it happens.
I'm hired.

My pimply manager
plays pocket-pool as
I bend to stock the shelves,
& at the register
an old bag calls me "the tubby one"
because I can't honour
her expired coupons.

Season's Greetings from
Your Hometown IGA

The month of December
teeming with testimonials:
tales of staff parties
passed from till to till
mythologizing the fevered
Boogie Nights of bag boys, cashiers.

Dwindled be the days spent
scanning, stocking, biding time
until break, bitching over smokes
& muffins about those ladies
& gentlemen who question
prices and addition. *Fuck em!*

This party will be swinging.

Hey, Santa will be there this year.
For a gag some gal might tug
his beard & the GM might giggle
about the days when boys'd
snap the back of her brassiere.

After a slippery number
of rums, Rodney will
get lucky in the backseat of
his Buick and talk of the gal
he's bagged–*skank, ho*–
will zing through every
aisle the the morning after.

But not before the sweaty
slow dancing, team-building cheers
presents, piñata, tears.
Then it's back to work.
Punching clock, pushing cart.
Cussing life, its dirty reason.

A Good
Testament
to the Drink

Talk is cheap
but it takes
money
to buy rum
& drink is
as good
as talk,
sometimes better,
& a bird
in the hand
is a bird
in the hand
but I never
met a bird
who could beat
a cold pint
& a pickled egg
in the heart
of your palm
after a long day
on the line
& it's a pisser
but there'll
always be
some unlucky
beggar, trudging

on his own two
monkey feet
the road home,
blood
on his sleeves,
but mostly
it's cow's
or pig's
or sheep's
some days
his own red grease
& I've never seen
a man the worse
for drink,
my Lady Love
will be ready
to kick my arse
if I don't get
my mosey on,
shaking
her fist at me,
shaking our babies
to sleep, my sup-sup
gone,
gobbled by the dog.
Three sheets to the wind
I am & oh my,
how she pins me up to dry.

It's All the Hair of the Dog
that Gets to You

It's been one humdinger of a shindig
if you find yourself, midway on Sunday,
heading for the tavern end of the road.
Lady Booze still marauding your organs,
time to murder the dirge of decorum:
uncoil the kinks, kick off yesterday's reek,
macerate with drink any puritanical stirrings.

Swiftly goes the blessed barmaid
with a run in her nude panty hose. Gimlet.
Bloody Mary. She's a siren, fixing elixir.
The broken vessels on your nose are a map
of the liquors that unburden your soul.
Pat down your pockets. *I'll take another.*
King of the Caesars, bar stool your throne.

Vance Romance, Karaoke King,
Live at The Bada-Bing: A Love Story

Sing it, Vance!

Rose swoons for her crooner, swings & sways
as he cruises the room, covering
a classic tune with sparkle & swagger.
Tonight, the bar's two-deep, crowd's rockin'.
Our Karaoke King reels them in
with a soloist's rendition, his Meatloaf
Special: *Paradise by the Dashboard Light.*

There's a blip in the sound, but our King
carries on, moonlighting, romancing
as the strobe spins its light. Old T-Bird
is canned, skunked, cartwheeling across
the floor while Romance takes ten, his gut
a strange fin, moving in, moving out.
To think that comely Rose covets him.

It's a good time 'til Hoochie Mama
shimmies on stage, claims Vance as her King.
He pinches her cheeks, twirls her around.
Rose throws back her drink, hikes up her skirt,
takes to the floor. She pummels the air.
Mama wiggles her hips & blows Rose
a kiss. Rose turns to her Vance, looks long

in his eyes. Taste of her lips. The flesh
of her full thighs. His Lady of Bail.
Her disappearance is his demise.
King rushes to the microphone, calls
Rose to his side. They sway to a slow
song. Vance sings for his flower, restores
her faith with a sultry number.

One Last Shot: A Lovelorn
Soul Testifies at His Local Saloon

He won't listen. I, however,
have been clear, not cruel. *No,*
says this barmaid. No sir. Cut
the tie that tethers your staid soul to me.
Drink up. Pay up. Go walk your woe.

(Will you bash my head against the rail?
Will you screw me up against the wall?)

Round it goes. Rings like the last-call
bell. Did I catch his coy
smile? Another gin?
                    Make it tall.
I'm no stalker. Not one for ploys.
Just you're so pretty. Smile & all.

(Feed me candy when I'm black & blue?
Buy me flowers when I say we're through?)

Wink. He's drooling.
I'll lose my mind.
His head, addled, is foul,
fetid. He asks me to be kind.
Again, I recoil. So I'm a sow,
cocktease. It's a fantastic bind.

(Can I strut my stuff in pleather & satin?
Can we drink a case, warm the mattress?)

Bad case of the stumbles, he's dead
to the world. *Tell me scram.*
Don't want me. Well, fuck you all.

                              Led
like a lion, I say to the lamb,
I can't lie with the man who begs to be bled.

Hey There Pretty Lady, *or*
The Three-Thirty Dirties

No two ways about it,
I'm liquored.

When the lights go up,
I know the stakes
are low, but he isn't half-bad.
Besides, I'm lonesome.
It's been a while.
I wouldn't mind a body to hold.

Outside, the fool's gold
of smoking street-dogs beckons.

He slides a hand into my back pocket,
kneading my ass as if dough.

Next stop is a donut shop
where I'm left alone.
While he's standing in the stall,
doing his damnedest to hit the bowl,
I can smell his dirty sheets,
hear my head hitting the headboard.

I book it home.

A Grand Affair, *or*
Bert Loves Carol as Much
as He Can When He Can

Va-Va-Va-Voom.

In walks Carol's
perfume. Shortly
thereafter comes Carol.

Bert plays it cool.

His heart's sprung eyes,
a musty spud revived.

It's their one night
a week. Half-price
wings, two carafes
& then afters.

Bert's late again.

His wife will be
waiting for him.

Carol understands.

Her panties
stuffed in her pocket.

GNOME, SWEET GNOME
(A SUITE OF POEMS)

Gnome, Sweet Gnome

Prelude

I shut my eyes and all the world drops dead;
I lift my lids and all is born again.
(I think I made you up inside my head.)
—SYLVIA PLATH

The name's Harry Humbolt.
I've always lived alone,
though there is a Gnome
I bought from Randy's Dollar Barn.
He's cast in concrete
& his cap is painted red.
He cuts the grass by moonlight.
A skunk sleeps at his feet.

My Gnome's gone missing.
Three whole days. Eternity.

Would you want to be my friend?

Harry & Gnome, Happier Days

Our squabble began with blunt scissors
& my Gentlemen's Choice hair dye.
I'd cut my locks around midnight,
covered my grey with black.
Gnome said I looked a country egg.
A bumpkin escaped from the pen.

"If I were a bird, I'd peck Harry.
Make him bleed. Scramble his guts
in a pan, string his giblets in the trees."

Crestfallen, I took a lasagna to bed.
When light broke like tine-pricked yolk,
Gnome was nowhere to be seen.

Day Four, Random Thoughts & Clues

That bastard might be alley-shacked,
eating day-olds with some bum,
but I doubt he's dawdled beyond
a block, not with his stumps.

Gnome was my soul subject,
without him I can't rule.
Our TV took her antennae off,
our goldfish jumped the bowl.

Dear Birdie, Shameless Tramp
& Neighbour, *or* Suspect #1

Girl who stole my Gnome of stone!
I've spied his cap upon your head.
At times a man can't quiet the edict
of imagination. I've seen him prancing
in your garden. I dream you dead
& buried. Shall I file your fingers,
teeth and toes against my revolving
grindstone? Bird-bird? Beauty?
I am no tawdry gimcrack. I am able.
I've a photo of you in my wallet.

Where Once

Where once I traced our shadows
& on the walls our puppets played,
our stage is but a graveyard.
His expert ghost my plague.
I wake to shapes of sadness
& suspect that during sleep,
a demon drags his digger,
thrusts it in me deep. Dancing
with a dirge that grinds, he packs
me full of dirt. A peony spreads
her perfect gills. I smell nothing but grief.

Ding-Dong

Last eve that harlot Birdie donned
Gnome's clogs. Played with reindeer
on my roof. One wink, I did not sleep.
I might've joined her party had I rightly
been addressed. Instead, I smoked
my lonely pipe. I slid under my bed.
Counted cobwebs & when they parted
winged rats costumed as kings spoke
in tongues. Gobbledegook! I understood:
"Great tribulation's at hand! Wrath
has come! Who is able to stand?"

I could not rise. Bedsprings overhead.
I thought of Gnome, his stoic stance.

Should I fetch my finest weeds?
Walk the lane? Ring Bird's bell?

Mine, Mine, Mine

Bird carried a spade. Bent, uprooted
a tuber. I walked toward her, arse
cheeks slippery with sweat. I puffed
my chest to hide the extra pounds.
(Stress, my friends. Stress.)
A tractor crawled into my head.
I tipped my cap, said, "Good day."
My Gnome was perched under
her mulberry. Starlings skirmished
in the sky. I swear, she looked me up
then down! I closed my eyes, saw tap
dancing titties. My cock smiled.

When I came to, she was inside.
Gnome leered. Contemptuous child.

Corporeal Friends
Are Spiritual Enemies

These fits of sadness
do not impair my judgement
but resemble madness.
I was not meant for touch.
My pen's been gnawed
to a nub. Black drool
straddles my bearded chin.
I am nobody's friend. Where
are the gates of paradise?
Lost & found in women
& in men? Gnome, why
surrender to some glitzy
girl? It's me who picked
you from the shelf,
freed you in my garden.

Let it alone, you say.

Go it alone. By oneself.
By one's lonesome.
Singly. Single. Unaided.
Unassisted. Solitary. Solus.

Harry lived alone.

LOVE, DELIVERANCE

Waking on the Docks, Honeymoon Over

Blue jeans tangled around my ankles, I sat up
to the swell-retreat of water sounding sometimes
like a frog's hiccup, then quickening to a thirsty,
lapping dog. The dock rocked as I haggled

with my limbs. I tipped the dregs of our love-
inducing potion into the lake, hawked a loogie
& lit a cigarette. We stalked the sleeping streets,
boy & me. If I wanted it to end, I still tried

to please, wore a wistful-girl compliance. We walked
past a cat slugged by fender sometime in the night,
its body seeping blood like a string-mop tearing water.
My boy laughed, said *cool.* I nodded, but later

signed the holy cross & I squinted as it danced
a black-ink hokey-pokey inside my head. We found
a table in Vern's Donut Villa. The radio blasted tunes
for the waitress who served us in a finger-snapping,

footloose frenzy & potato-chip-shaped ladies lit
one off the other. Their perfume & pink lipstick
made me queasy, but I smiled, lip splitting, chapped
from all-night kissing. Boy vomited on the table.

A muffler grumbled in the lot. We stared at it, avoiding.
I broke a day-old donut, tossed to the flocking gulls.

Ode to Dirty Donnie, *or* Nic Fit

Shot through the heart, and you're to blame.
Darling, you give love a bad name.
—Bon Jovi

A gift slipped through the diamond eye
of chain-link fence. Filterless. Home-rolled
by Sacred Heart's sexiest Metal Head.
Sucked to butt, pinked by lips glossed
Troublegum, I flicked you from my index
& my thumb. A schoolgirl trick. I watched
you arc in the air, crash-burn on hoary ground.

Hooked. My body a haven for Craven-As.
Smoke-rings hung like halos over my head.
You, my loathsome lover blistered my lips,
dragged me from bed before the alarm.
Empty. Obsessed. I scavenged under couch
cushions for coins. A goner from the first
pull. I couldn't quit on you, my beau.

Shotgun Wedding

All rapture foregone. The forecast, gloomy.
I coiled, coiffed my bridesmaid's bouffant.

Next, we put you into the gown. One leg, the other.
You waded into its round white mouth.

Thereafter, a swatch of white roamed the room,
loomed, a golem, not the girl I knew.

Devoured by rasping, sequined satin,
I half-anticipated you'd chew your way out.

Instead, we guffawed. I passed the bottle
& we agreed one nip couldn't hurt.

❋

At City Hall we turned the pages of a greasy
black binder & picked a prayer for love. Your groom

was running late. A skeet of a woman shot by us,
wondering aloud, *Which way for dog tags?*

The JP wore too much rouge. Her clownish spiel
more caveat than confirmation & you might've drifted

skyward, hot air puffing up your dress, had your mate
not slipped the metal band on, anchored you.

＊

A Red Top taxi idled in the lot. Your carriage.
His slew of buddies waited by the curb: round

of high-fives, a 2-4 for the trip, liquid honeymoon.
A shy bouquet of roses chucked into gangly shrubbery.

You both waved from the rear window
as the car lurched into traffic. Newlyweds.

Past Courtship, *or* When Can We Split?

If I'm tense & ticking, will you mix me a drink?
  Yes, I'll bring you a bottle
  & our glasses will chink.

Will you still love me if I grow fat?
  Come, night is our fairground,
  let's not have a spat.

Will your folks adore me if I wear this dress?
  You look a wind-wrecked wench,
  but, Love, be my guest.

Let's say I do murder & cops ask you to plea?
  Lady, I'll point in your direction,
  then I'll flee.

When pigeons bomb our roost at break of day,
Will you kiss me on the cheek, beg me stay?
  No, I'll ask you to bend over,
  I'll screw you mighty hard,
  I'll bid you pack your baggage,
  & hide my credit card.

Put Me to Bed...

Sally, all the booze
is gone, beauty. I won't go before

it's done, lady. Let me have it
while it's here. I might

have to wake, someday.
Will you wait here with me?

Just one more drink.
I need to hear this song.

Heartbroken Man Places
Entire Life on Hold

It is March. You are heartbroken.
You are alone & by alone I mean
everything reminds you of her:
the carton of curdled skim milk
in the otherwise empty fridge remains
because you cannot bear to make it trash.
The carton is bloated & your heart has gone
sour. The apartment is hot because you cannot
get off the couch to pull the cord. The fan
has a dusty mask you should be wearing.
You are bloated. There is dead milk
in the fridge. You are thinking about dusting
with your old underwear, wearing the pair
she left behind. Gusset of cotton, otherwise
cheap peach satin. It is March. You are broken.
There are people who might pay
good money to make you smile.

And Once Again

I've failed. At love.
I stayed away while he packed.
Came home to broken glass,
plaster dust. The shower curtain
missing. Hooks too.
I won't give the rundown.
Empty. Except for the puke
in the kitchen sink.
A turd in the toilet,
his final farewell.

Every corner of me in need
of caulking, or cock.
Some quick fix like booze
and a blinding headache.

The Happy Ending

deflates after I've paid.
She smelled of chlorine.
Her name was Fantasia.

On my way home to you
I want to strangle my brain.
My cock is still wet.
It is raining & I cannot explain.

Love Agapic & Erotic
(Between Friends)

What gives? Our love confused,
trapped between agapic & erotic.

I am bound to someone else.

What we need is platonic love,
settled friendship to oust
us from our dovetailed folly.

I breathe in the forbidden.
It is you. My flesh is riven.
We lay in grass, count
the passing, endless clouds.
You revive my skin with your cruel
touch & when we rise,
is it your imprint or mine?

I have met your wife.

Love agapic, selfless, gaping.
Love erotic, where we are tangled, taking.

Please Don't Die on Me Now

Driving uphill in a car we call Mildred.
She's failing. He's ten & two steering,
muttering a refrain "Please don't die
on me now. Don't die. Not now."

Mildred is old & likely deaf. Give it a rest,
I think. It's been tense the whole ride.
His hands on the wheel are gleaming. He's had
his fingers in the chip bag all morning.

I side with Mildred because at least she's trying.
He might be beside me in this crap car that smells
of gasoline & nacho cheese, but we're both impatient.
I need out. He wants to clock 100 on the highway.

"Don't die on me now baby." He cracks
a can of pop. The stereo's been busted for months.
A field of white turbines in front of us appears
to be endless, every blade at a standstill.

After You Bailed

Gilled & gutted, I knocked boots
with a numbskull fishmonger.
        To no avail.

Rigs, jigs, spinners, spoons,
plugs, bugs, hook & shank,
none can keep me true.
Your effigy burns,
a stigma inside my lids.
Your lips, your kiss.

After you sailed,
I curled up in a bottle,
a fetal, skeletal ship adrift
in her boozy slumber, lariat
hung around my neck.
You pulled me under. I spied her,
your finer model: handcrafted,
gilt, blessed by the artisan's touch.

After we failed, I failed. Yes,
it's laughable. Pain can be laudable.
Cut the motor & cup a hand
to your ear. Hear my misery
skip across the lake. Hurrah! Aha!

        How could you?
        Ah, piss.

Thanks

Paul and Mary Lou Strimas. Norma Strimas.
Melisa, Jackie, Jillian and Shepherd Strimas. Josh Richardson. Russell Ackerman.

My relatives, the Strimas and Thompson families.

Michael and Barry Callaghan and the wonderful people at Exile Editions.

Karen Solie, who edited this book.

Priscila Uppal and Christopher Doda, dear friends and proofreaders.

Jeannette Lorito, who designed the cover of this book and provided the photo from her collection. Please visit www.jlorito.com

Mark Tearle, who took my author photo.

Alison Jones and Attila Berki for supporting me. I am lucky to know people like you.

Catherine Bush, and all of the writers who are now studying at, or who have graduated from, the University of Guelph's Creative Writing MFA program. Love and thanks to Janice Kulyk Keefer, Dionne Brand and Judith Thompson.

Connie Rooke, now departed, you gave me so much.

I am privileged to have many fabulous friends. In particular, Krista Brodhurst, Evie Christie, Bonnie Maitland, Elisabeth di Mariaffi, Leigh Nash, Andrew Faulkner and Stuart Ross.

Thanks, too, to Michael and Linda. And Tulin Valeri and Patsy McLean.

Bates Strimas, you are a gem!

The Ontario Council for the Arts Writers' Reserve program has generously supported my writing, as has The Canada Council for the Arts. Huge thanks to Brick Books (Kitty and John), Cormorant Books (Marc) and *Taddle Creek* (Conan).

Also, Margo Swiss and David Kent who head the St. Thomas Poetry Series.

Earlier versions of these poems have appeared in *Exile: The Literary Quarterly, The Wascana Review, Taddle Creek, The Globe & Mail.com* and the anthology *Poetry as Liturgy.*

Finally, all my love and gratitude to Nathan Whitlock and his children, Iago and Olive.

Notes

The epigraph for this book is taken from Elizabeth Bishop's poem "One Art" (*The Complete Poems: 1927 - 1979*, Farrar, Straus and Giroux).

The quote used in my poem "Love's Reprobate" is taken from Andrew Motion's poem "A Dying Race" (*Selected Poems 1976 - 1997*, Faber & Faber).

The Sylvia Plath's excerpt in "Gnome, Sweet Gnome" is from her poem "Mad Girl's Love Song."

The lines "These fits of saddness / do not impair my judgement / but resemble maddness" found in "Corporeal Friends Are Spiritual Enemies" are a gloss of similar lines originally penned by Gerard Manley Hopkins.

Meaghan Strimas lives in Toronto, where she works at *Quill & Quire* magazine and for the University of Guelph's Creative Writing MFA program. Strimas is the editor of *The Selected Gwendolyn MacEwen*, and the author of one previous collection of poetry, *Junkman's Daughter*.

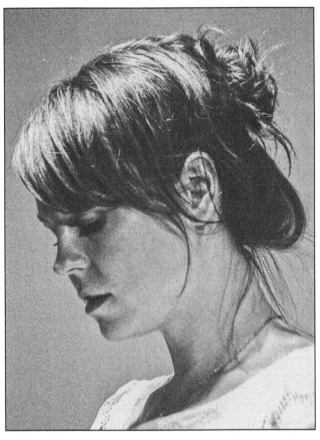

Photograph by Mark Tearle